Design: Jill Coote
Recipe Photography: Peter Barry
Recipe styling: Jacqueline Bellefontaine,
Bridgeen Deery and Wendy Devenish
Jacket and Illustration Artwork: Jane Winton,
courtesy of Bernard Thornton Artists, London
Editorial: Laura Potts

CLB 3354
Published by Grange Books,
an imprint of Grange Books Limited,
The Grange, Grange Yard, London.
© 1993 CLB Publishing,
Godalming, Surrey, England.
All rights reserved.
Printed and bound in Singapore
This edition reprinted in 1994
ISBN 1-85627-309-1

THE LITTLE BOOK · OF ·

Chinese

RECIPES

*The perfect introduction to one of the
world's oldest and most respected culinary
traditions.*

Grange BOOKS

Introduction

$\mathcal{T}$ he Chinese, like the French, are a nation of food lovers, and the preparation and enjoyment of food plays a central part in their way of life. The Chinese culinary tradition, one of the oldest in the world, now enjoys an almost unprecedented popularity in the West.

Stir-frying is the most commonly used technique in Chinese cookery and is one with which many people are familiar. This method of cooking though not difficult to master is a skill and a few simple rules need to be followed in order to get the best results.

Successful stir-fry dishes rely, in large part, on careful preparation. By chopping or shredding ingredients, a greater surface area is created, which in turn reduces the amount of cooking time required. Care should be taken to ensure that each of the ingredients is cut to roughly the same size. As stir-frying will often take just a few minutes, it is vital to have all the ingredients pre-prepared and the necessary sauces to hand. This helps to avoid last-minute panic, and so helps prevent over-cooking.

Secondly, because stir-frying is so quick and uses such a direct source of heat, it is important to use only the finest ingredients. Texture and taste are fundamental to good Chinese cookery and poor quality ingredients cannot be successfully "hidden". This general rule applies to all ingredients in a recipe, but is particularly important when choosing cuts of meat. Although marinades usually act as a tenderiser, they cannot perform miracles. Cheap cuts, which need long, slow cooking to break down the tissues, will remain tough if they are stir-fried. In traditional Chinese cookery, meat or fish are used in small amounts, but are used to maximum effect. This emphasis on quality rather than quantity means that the best cuts can be bought while still keeping the overall cost of the dish quite low.

Stir-fry dishes can be cooked in an ordinary frying pan, but better results will usually be achieved in a wok. Its gently sloping sides retain the heat far more effectively than a conventional frying pan whilst providing a larger surface area on which to cook the food. When cooking, the wok should be heated, and then the temperature reduced before adding the oil. If the wok is too hot the oil will burn, giving a charred, oily taste to the food. The heat should be progressively raised for the addition of other ingredients, unless otherwise specified in the recipe.

The recipes in this book cover a broad cross-section of Chinese stir-fry dishes and provide ideas for the rice or noodle dishes to serve with them. The step-by-step recipes are easy to follow and provide the perfect introduction to one of world's oldest and most respected culinary traditions, helping you to recreate the tastes of authentic Chinese cuisine in your own home.

Wonton Soup

SERVES 6-8

The recipe for this classic Chinese soup uses pre-made wonton wrappers.

PREPARATION: 25-30 mins
COOKING: 5-10 mins

20-24 wonton wrappers
2 tbsps chopped Chinese parsley
90g/3oz finely minced chicken or pork
3 spring onions, finely chopped
2.5cm/1 inch piece fresh ginger, peeled and
    grated
1 egg, lightly beaten
1.5 litres/2½ pints chicken stock
15ml/1 tbsp dark soy sauce
Dash sesame oil
Salt and pepper
Chinese parsley or watercress for garnish

Step 2 Place a spoonful of filling on half of each wrapper

Step 3 Fold over the tops and press firmly with the fingers to seal.

1. Place all the wonton wrappers on a large, flat surface. Mix together the chicken or pork, chopped parsley, spring onions and ginger. Brush the edges of the wrappers lightly with beaten egg.

2. Place a small mound of mixture on one half of the wrappers and fold the other half over the top to form a triangle.

3. Press with the fingers to seal the edges well.

4. Bring the stock to the boil in a large saucepan. Add the filled wontons and simmer 5-10 minutes or until they float to the surface. Add remaining ingredients to the soup and garnish.

Spiced Fried Soup

SERVES 4

A delicious, nutritious soup which is a meal in itself.

PREPARATION: 20 mins
COOKING: 20-25 mins

4-8 tbsps oil
1 clove garlic, peeled but left whole
450g/1lb chicken breast, skinned, boned and
  cut into small pieces
1 cake tofu, drained and cut into 2.5cm/1 inch
  cubes
60g/2oz raw cashew nuts
4 shallots, roughly chopped
1 carrot, thinly sliced
90g/3oz mange tout
60g/2oz Chinese noodles, soaked for 5 minutes
  in hot water and drained thoroughly
1.5 litres/2½ pints vegetable or chicken stock
Juice of 1 lime
¼ tsp turmeric
2 curry leaves
1 tsp grated fresh ginger
1 tbsp soy sauce
Salt and pepper

1. Heat some of the oil in a wok or large frying
pan. Add the garlic and cook until brown.
Remove from the pan and discard.

2. Add the chicken pieces and cook in the oil,
until they begin to brown. Remove and drain well.

Step 2 Stir-fry the chicken pieces in hot oil until they begin to brown.

3. Add a little more oil and cook the tofu until
lightly brown. Remove and drain well.

4. Add the cashews and cook, stirring
constantly until toasted. Remove and drain well.

5. Add a little more oil and fry the shallots and
carrots until lightly browned. Stir in the mange
tout and cook for 1 minute. Remove from the
pan and drain.

6. Heat the remaining oil until it is very hot. Add
the noodles and cook quickly until brown on one
side. Turn over and brown the other side.

7. Lower the heat and pour in the stock. Stir in
the remaining ingredients. Cover and simmer
gently for 10 minutes, stirring occasionally.

8. Add the fried ingredients and heat through
for 5 minutes. Serve immediately.

Barbecued Spareribs

SERVES 4-6

These tasty spare ribs can be served either as a starter or as part of a larger meal.

PREPARATION: 45 mins, plus 1 hr to marinate the
    ribs. 4 hrs to soak the spring onion garnish
COOKING: 1 hr

1.8kg/4lbs fresh spare ribs
3 tbsps dark soy sauce
6 tbsps hoisin sauce
2 tbsps dry sherry
¼ tsp five spice powder
1 tbsp brown sugar
4-6 spring onions for garnish

---

1. Trim the root ends and the dark green tops
from the onions.

2. Cut both ends into thin strips, leaving about
1.25cm/½ inch in the middle uncut.

Step 2 Cut both ends of the onions into thin strips, leaving the middle whole.

Step 3 Place in ice water and leave to stand 4 hours or overnight until the ends curl.

3. Place in ice water for several hours or
overnight for the ends to curl up.

4. Cut the spareribs into one-rib pieces. Mix all
the remaining ingredients together, pour over
the ribs and stir to coat evenly. Allow to stand
for 1 hour.

5. Put the sparerib pieces on a rack in a
roasting pan containing 570ml/1 pint water and
cook in a preheated 180°C/350°F/Gas Mark 4
oven for 30 minutes. Add more hot water to the
pan while cooking, if necessary.

6. Turn the ribs over and brush with the
remaining sauce. Cook 30 minutes longer, or
until tender. Serve garnished with the spring
onion brushes.

Quick Fried Prawns

SERVES 4-6

This easy to cook recipe can be prepared with either raw or cooked prawns.

PREPARATION: 30 mins for the prawns to
    marinate
COOKING: 2 mins

900g/2lbs cooked prawns in their shells
2 cloves garlic, crushed
2.5cm/1 inch piece fresh ginger, finely
    chopped
1 tbsp chopped fresh Chinese parsley
    (coriander)
3 tbsps oil
1 tbsp rice wine or dry sherry
1½ tbsps light soy sauce
Chopped spring onions to garnish

1. Shell the prawns except for the very tail ends. Place the prawns in a bowl with the remaining ingredients, except for the garnish, and leave to marinate for 30 minutes.

2. Heat the wok and add the prawns and their marinade. Stir-fry briefly to heat the cooked prawns.

Step 1
Carefully pull the head of the prawn away from the body.

3. Chop the onions roughly. Sprinkle over the prawns and serve immediately.

Step 2 Peel the shells from the prawns, leaving only the tail ends on.

Prawn Egg Fried Rice

SERVES 6

This rice dish is substantial enough to eat as a meal on its own

PREPARATION: 20 mins
COOKING: 15 mins

450g/1lb long grain rice
2 eggs
½ tsp salt
4 tbsps oil
2 spring onions, chopped
1 large onion, chopped
2 cloves of garlic, chopped
120g/4oz small prawns, peeled
60g/2oz shelled peas
2 tbsps dark soy sauce

---

1. Wash the rice thoroughly and put it in a saucepan. Add water to come 2.5cm/1 inch above the top of the rice.

Step 3 Rinse the rice in cold water and separate the grains with a fork.

Step 4 Cook the eggs with the onions gently, until set and softly scrambled.

2. Bring the rice to the boil, stir once, then reduce the heat. Cover and simmer until the liquid has been absorbed.

3. Rinse the rice in cold water and separate the grains with a fork.

4. Beat the eggs with a pinch of salt. Heat 1 tablespoon of the oil in a wok and cook the spring onions and the onions until soft. Pour in the egg and stir gently, until the mixture is set. Remove the egg mixture and set it aside.

5. Heat a further tablespoon of the oil and fry the garlic, prawns and peas for 2 minutes. Remove and set aside.

6. Heat the remaining oil in the wok and stir in the rice and salt. Stir-fry, to heat the rice through, then add the egg and the shrimp mixtures and the soy sauce. Serve immediately.

Fried Rice

SERVES 6-8

The traditional Chinese accompaniment to stir-fried dishes.

PREPARATION: 30 mins
COOKING: 4 mins

450g/1lb cooked rice, well drained and dried
3 tbsps oil
1 egg, beaten
1 tbsp soy sauce
60g/2oz cooked peas
2 spring onions, thinly sliced
Dash sesame oil
Salt and pepper

Step 2 Stir to coat the rice with egg, and toss mixture over heat to separate grains of rice.

Step 2 Add rice and peas on top of egg mixture.

1. Heat a wok and add the oil. Pour in the egg and soy sauce and cook until just beginning to set.

2. Add the rice and peas and stir to coat with the egg mixture. Allow to cook for about 3 minutes, stirring continuously. Add seasoning and sesame oil.

3. Spoon into a serving dish and sprinkle over the spring onions.

Stir-Fry Noodles

SERVES 4

This enticing recipe is easy to prepare and makes an ideal supper dish.

PREPARATION: 20 mins
COOKING: 15 mins

225g/8oz fine egg noodles
4 tbsps peanut oil
1 onion, finely chopped
2 cloves garlic, crushed
1 green chilli, seeded and finely sliced
1 tsp chilli paste
120g/4oz pork, finely sliced
2 sticks of celery, sliced
¼ small cabbage, finely shredded
1 tbsp light soy sauce
120g/4oz prawns, shelled and deveined
Salt and pepper

Step 1 Soak the noodles in hot water for 5 minutes, until they are soft. Rinse in cold water and drain thoroughly in a colander.

Step 4 Stir-fry the pork, celery and cabbage with the onion mixture for 3 minutes, or until the pork is cooked through.

1. Soak the noodles in hot water for 5 minutes, until they are soft. Rinse in cold water and drain thoroughly in a colander.

2. Heat the oil in a wok and stir-fry the onion, garlic and chilli, until the onion is soft and just golden brown.

3. Add the chilli paste and stir well.

4. Add the pork, celery and cabbage and stir-fry for about 3 minutes, or until the pork is cooked through. Season to taste.

5. Stir in the soy sauce, noodles and prawns, tossing the mixture together thoroughly and heating through before serving.

Sweet and Sour Pork

SERVES 2-4
This popular dish originated in Canton.

PREPARATION: 15 mins
COOKING: 15 mins

120g/4oz plain flour
4 tbsps cornflour
1½ tsps baking powder
Pinch salt
1 tbsp oil
Water
225g/8oz pork fillet, cut into 1.25cm/½ inch cubes
1 onion, sliced
1 green pepper, seeded, cored and sliced
1 small can pineapple chunks, juice reserved
Oil for frying

Sweet and Sour Sauce
2 tbsps cornflour
120g/4oz light brown sugar
Pinch salt
120ml/4 fl oz cider vinegar or rice vinegar
1 clove garlic, crushed
1 tsp root ginger, grated
6 tbsps tomato ketchup
6 tbsps reserved pineapple juice

1. Sift the flour, cornflour, baking powder and salt into a bowl. Add the oil and enough water to make a thick, smooth batter. Beat until smooth.

Step 2 Dip the pork cubes into the batter and then drop into hot oil.

2. Heat enough oil in a wok to deep-fry the pork. Dip the pork cubes into the batter and drop into the hot oil. Fry 4-5 pieces of pork at a time and remove them with a draining spoon to paper towels. Continue until all the pork is fried.

3. Pour off most of the oil from the wok and add the sliced onion, pepper and pineapple. Cook over high heat for 1-2 minutes. Remove and set aside.

4. Mix all the sauce ingredients together and pour into the wok. Bring slowly to the boil, stirring continuously until thickened. Allow to simmer for about 1-2 minutes or until completely clear.

5. Add the vegetables, pineapple and pork to the sauce and stir well. Reheat for 1-2 minutes and serve immediately.

Pork Chow Mein

SERVES 4

Sliced beef or chicken can also be used in this classic Chinese dish.

PREPARATION: 20 mins
COOKING: 20 mins

275g/10oz egg noodles
1 tbsp Chinese wine, or dry sherry
1 tbsp light soy sauce
1 tsp sugar
450g/1lb pork fillet, thinly sliced
3 tbsps oil
1 tsp grated root ginger
1 stick celery, sliced diagonally
1 leek, finely sliced
1 red pepper, cored, seeded and cut into strips
1 small can bamboo shoots, sliced
140ml/¼ pint stock
30g/1oz peas
1 tsp cornflour
1 tbsp water
Salt and pepper

---

1. Soak the noodles in hot water for 5 minutes, then rinse in cold water and drain thoroughly.

2. Combine the wine, soy sauce and sugar in a large bowl. Add the pork, mix well, and leave to marinate for 15 minutes.

3. Heat the oil in a large wok, and add the ginger, celery and leek. Stir-fry for 2 minutes.

4. Add the red pepper and bamboo shoots and stir-fry for a further 2 minutes.

Step 4 Add the red pepper and bamboo shoots and stir-fry for a further 2 minutes.

5. Remove the vegetables from the wok. Increase the heat and add the pork, reserving the marinade. Stir-fry for 4 minutes, or until cooked through.

6. Return the vegetables to the wok, mixing with the pork. Add the stock gradually, stirring well.

7. Add the peas and cook for 2 minutes.

8. Mix the cornflour with the water, add to the marinade and stir in well.

9. Stir the marinade sauce into the vegetables and pork in the wok. Mix well, until the sauce is thickened and smooth. Add the noodles and stir everything together thoroughly until it has heated through.

10. Season to taste and simmer for 3 minutes before serving.

Stir-Fried Calves' Liver with Peppers and Carrots

SERVES 4

Quick stir-frying ensures that the calves' liver remains pink and tender inside.

PREPARATION: 15-20 mins
COOKING: 10-12 mins

2 tbsps oil
1 onion, thinly sliced
1 clove garlic, finely sliced
600g/1¼lbs calves' liver, cut into thin strips
2 tbsps seasoned wholemeal flour
4 tbsps dry sherry
140ml/¼ pint water, or vegetable stock
1 green pepper, seeded and cut into thin strips
3 large carrots, cut into strips
Salt and pepper
120g/4oz bean sprouts

Step 2 Roll the strips of calves' liver in the seasoned flour, until they are evenly coated.

Step 5 Stir in the bean sprouts and heat through for about 1 minute, until they are warm, but still crunchy.

1. Heat the oil in a wok and stir-fry the onion and garlic for 3 minutes.

2. Roll the strips of liver in the seasoned flour and add to the wok, along with the onion. Stir-fry quickly, until the liver is sealed on the outside, but is still pink in the centre.

3. Stir in the sherry and bring to a rapid boil. Add the water, or stock, along with the green pepper, carrots and seasoning to taste.

4. Stir-fry the liver in the sauce for 3 minutes, over a high heat.

5. Add the bean sprouts to the wok and stir-fry for 1 minute then serve.

Shredded Beef with Vegetables

SERVES 4

Red and green chilli peppers give an extra kick to this tasty stir-fry

PREPARATION: 15 mins
COOKING: 10 mins

225g/8oz lean beef steak, cut into thin strips
½ tsp salt
4 tbsps vegetable oil
1 red and 1 green chilli pepper, seeded and
    sliced into strips
1 tsp vinegar
1 stick celery, cut into thin strips
2 carrots, cut into thin strips
1 leek, white part only, sliced into thin strips
2 cloves garlic, finely chopped
1 tbsp light soy sauce
1 tbsp dark soy sauce
2 tsps Chinese wine, or dry sherry
1 tsp caster sugar
½ tsp freshly ground black pepper

1. Put the strips of beef into a large bowl and sprinkle with the salt. Rub the salt into the meat and allow to stand for 5 minutes.

2. Heat 1 tbsp of the oil in a large wok. When the oil begins to smoke, reduce the heat and stir in the beef and the chillies. Stir-fry for 4-5 minutes.

3. Add the remaining oil and continue stir-frying the beef, until it turns crispy.

Step 1 Rub the salt well into the sliced beef and leave to stand.

4. Add the vinegar and stir until it evaporates, then add the celery, carrots, leek and garlic. Stir-fry for 2 minutes.

5. Mix together the soy sauces, wine or sherry, sugar and pepper. Pour this mixture over the beef and cook for 2 minutes. Serve immediately.

Step 5 Pour in the soy sauce mixture and stir-fry rapidly for about 2 minutes, making sure that the beef and vegetables are well coated.

Spiced Beef

SERVES 4

Ground star anise and fennel bring a hint of liquorice to this fragrant, spicy stir-fry.

PREPARATION: 30 mins
COOKING: 5-6 mins

450g/1lb fillet of beef
1 tsp soft brown sugar
2-3 star anise, ground
½ tsp ground fennel
1 tbsp dark soy sauce
2.5cm/1-inch piece fresh root ginger, grated
½ tsp salt
2 tbsps oil
6 spring onions, sliced
1 tbsp light soy sauce
½ tsp freshly ground black pepper

---

1. Cut the beef into thin strips 2.5cm/1 inch long, cutting across the grain of the meat.

2. Mix the sugar, spices and dark soy sauce in a bowl.

Step 5 Stir-fry the beef with the spring onions for 4 minutes.

3. Add the beef, ginger and salt and stir well to coat evenly. Cover and allow to stand for 20 minutes.

4. Heat the oil in a wok and stir-fry the onions for 1 minute.

5. Add the beef and fry, stirring constantly, for 4 minutes, or until the meat is well browned.

6. Stir in the light soy sauce and black pepper and cook gently for a further 1 minute.

Beef with Broccoli

SERVES 2-3

Cutting the meat across the grain ensures that it will be tender and will cook quickly.

PREPARATION: 25 mins
COOKING: 4 mins

450g/1lb rump steak, partially frozen
4 tbsps dark soy sauce
1 tbsp cornflour
1 tbsp dry sherry
1 tsp sugar
225g/8oz fresh broccoli
6 tbsps oil
2.5cm/1 inch piece ginger, peeled and
 shredded
Salt and pepper

---

1. Trim any fat from the meat and cut into very thin strips across the grain.

Step 1 Use partially frozen meat and slice it thinly across the grain.

Step 3 Cut the broccoli stalks in thin diagonal slices.

2. Combine the meat with the soy sauce, cornflour, sherry and sugar. Stir well and leave long enough for the meat to completely defrost.

3. Cut the broccoli into even-sized florets. Peel the stalks of the broccoli and cut into thin, diagonal slices.

4. Heat 2 tbsps of the oil in a wok. Add the broccoli and sprinkle with salt. Stir-fry until the broccoli is dark green. Do not cook for longer than 2 minutes. Remove from the wok and set aside.

5. Place the remaining oil in the wok and add the ginger and beef. Stir-fry for about 2 minutes. Return the broccoli to the pan and mix well. Heat through for 30 seconds then serve.

Chicken with Walnuts and Celery

SERVES 4

Oyster sauce lends a subtle, slightly salty taste to this Cantonese dish.

PREPARATION: 20 mins
COOKING: 8 mins

225g/8oz boned chicken, cut into 2.5cm/1 inch
 pieces
2 tsps soy sauce
2 tsps brandy
1 tsp cornflour
Salt and pepper
2 tbsps oil
1 clove garlic, left whole
120g/4oz walnut halves
3 sticks celery, cut in diagonal slices
140ml/¼ pint chicken stock
2 tsps oyster sauce

Step 3 Add the walnuts to the wok and cook until they are crisp.

Step 4 Use a large, sharp knife to cut the celery on the diagonal into thin slices.

1. Combine the chicken with the soy sauce, brandy, cornflour, salt and pepper.

2. Heat a wok and add the oil and garlic. Cook the garlic for about 1 minute to flavour the oil then remove.

3. Add the chicken in two batches. Stir-fry quickly without allowing the chicken to brown. Remove the chicken and add the walnuts to the wok. Cook for about 2 minutes until they are slightly brown.

4. Slice the celery, add to the wok and cook for 1 minute. Add the oyster sauce and stock and bring to the boil. When boiling, return the chicken to the pan and stir well. Serve immediately.

Singapore Fish

SERVES 6

The cuisine of Singapore was much influenced by that of China. In turn, the Chinese brought ingredients like curry powder into their own cuisine.

PREPARATION: 25 mins
COOKING: 10 mins

450g/1lb whitefish fillets
1 egg white
1 tbsp cornflour
2 tsps white wine
Salt and pepper
Oil for frying
1 large onion, coarsely chopped
1 tbsp mild curry powder
1 small tin pineapple pieces, drained and juice reserved
1 small tin mandarin orange segments, drained and juice reserved
1 small tin sliced water chesnuts, drained
1 tbsp cornflour
Juice of 1 lime
2 tsps sugar (optional)
Pinch salt and pepper

1. Starting at the tail end of the fillets, skin them using a sharp knife.

2. Slide the knife back and forth along the length of each fillet, pushing the fish flesh along as you go.

3. Cut the fish into even-sized pieces, about 5cm/2 inches.

Step 2 Hold filleting knife at a slight angle and slide knife along length of fillet in a sawing motion.

4. Mix together the egg white, cornflour, wine, salt and pepper. Place the fish in the mixture and leave to stand while heating the oil.

5. When the oil is hot, fry a few pieces of fish at a time until golden brown and crisp. Remove the fish to paper towels to drain once it is cooked.

6. Remove all but 1 tbsp of the oil from the wok and add the onion. Stir-fry for 1-2 minutes and add the curry powder. Cook for a further 1-2 minutes. Add the juice from the tinned fruit and bring to the boil.

7. Combine the cornflour and lime juice and add a spoonful of the boiling fruit juice. Return the mixture to the wok and cook until thickened. Taste and add sugar if desired. Add the fruit, water chesnuts and fried fish to the wok and stir to coat. Heat through 1 minute and serve immediately.

Kung Pao Prawns with Cashew Nuts

SERVES 6

This easy dish combines many different textures and tastes.

PREPARATION: 20 mins
COOKING: 3 mins

½ tsp chopped fresh ginger
1 tsp chopped garlic
1½ tbsps cornflour
¼ tsp bicarbonate of soda
Salt and pepper
¼ tsp sugar
450g/1lb uncooked prawns
4 tbsps oil
1 small onion, cut into dice
1 large or 2 small courgettes, coarsely chopped
1 small red pepper, coarsely chopped
60g/2oz cashew nuts

Sauce
180ml/6 fl oz chicken stock
1 tbsp cornflour
2 tsps chilli sauce
2 tsps bean paste (optional)
2 tsps sesame oil
1 tbsp dry sherry or rice wine

1. Mix together the ginger, garlic, cornflour, bicarbonate of soda, salt, pepper and sugar.

2. If the prawns are unpeeled, remove the peels and the dark vein. If large, cut in half. Place in the dry ingredients and leave to stand for 20 minutes.

Step 4 To dice the courgettes quickly, top and tail and cut into strips.

3. Heat the oil in a wok and when hot add the prawns. Stir-fry for about 20 seconds, or just until the prawns change colour. Transfer to a plate.

4. Add the onion to the same oil and cook for about 1 minute. Add the courgettes and red pepper and cook about 30 seconds.

5. Mix the sauce ingredients together and add to the wok. Cook, stirring constantly, until the sauce is thickened. Add the prawns and the cashew nuts and heat through.

Step 4 Cut the strips across with a large sharp knife into pieces.

Special Mixed Vegetables

SERVES 4

This dish illustrates the basic stir-frying technique for vegetables.

PREPARATION: 25 mins
COOKING: 3 mins

1 tbsp oil
1 clove garlic, crushed
2.5cm/1 inch piece root ginger, sliced
4 Chinese leaves, shredded
60g/2oz flat mushrooms, thinly sliced
60g/2oz bamboo shoots, sliced
3 sticks celery, diagonally sliced
60g/2oz baby corn, cut in half if large
1 small red pepper, thinly sliced
60g/2oz bean sprouts
2 tbsps light soy sauce
Dash sesame oil
Salt and pepper
3 tomatoes, peeled, seeded and quartered

Step Place in cold water to stop the cooking. The skin will then peel away easily.

Step 2 To peel the tomatoes, place them first in a pan of boiling water for 5 seconds. Tomatoes that are very ripe need less time.

1. Heat the oil in a wok and add the ingredients in the order given, reserving the tomatoes until last.

2. To make it easier to peel the tomatoes, remove the stems and place in boiling water for 5 seconds.

3. Remove from the boiling water and place in a bowl of cold water. This will make the peels easier to remove. Cut out the core end.

4. Cut the tomatoes in half and then in quarters and remove the seeds.

5. Cook the vegetables for about 2 minutes. Stir in the soy sauce and sesame oil and add the tomatoes. Heat through for 30 seconds and serve immediately.

Stir-Fry Tofu Salad

SERVES 4-6

Ideal for vegetarians, but so delicious that it will be enjoyed by everyone.

PREPARATION: 25 mins
COOKING: 2-4 mins

1 cake of tofu
120g/4oz mange tout
60g/2oz mushrooms
2 carrots, peeled
2 sticks celery
60g/2oz broccoli florets
140ml/¼ pint vegetable oil
3 tbsps lemon juice
2 tsps honey
1 tsp grated fresh ginger
3 tbsps soy sauce
Dash of sesame oil
4 spring onions
60g/2oz unsalted roasted peanuts
120g/4oz bean sprouts
½ head Chinese leaves

1. Drain the tofu well and press gently to remove any excess moisture. Cut into cubes.

2. Trim the tops and tails from the mange tout.

3. Thinly slice the mushrooms with a sharp knife.

4. Cut the carrots and celery into thin slices.

5. Trim the spring onions and slice them.

6. Heat 2 tbsps of the vegetable oil in a wok.

Step 4 Cut the vegetables with your knife at an angle to produce diagonal pieces.

Stir in the mange tout, mushrooms, celery, carrots and broccoli, and cook for 2 minutes, stirring constantly.

7. Remove the vegetables from the wok and set them aside to cool.

8. Put the remaining oil into a small bowl and whisk in the lemon juice, honey, ginger, soy sauce and sesame oil.

9. Stir the spring onions, peanuts and bean sprouts into the cooled vegetables.

10. Mix the dressing into the vegetables, then add the tofu, tossing it carefully so that it does not break up.

11. Shred the Chinese leaves and arrange them on a serving platter. Pile the salad ingredients over the top and serve well chilled.

Index

Barbecued Spareribs 12
Beef with Broccoli 32
Chicken with Walnuts and Celery 34
Fish and Seafood:
    Kung Pao Prawns with Cashew Nuts 38
    Quick Fried Prawns 14
    Singapore Fish 36
    Stir-Fry Noodles 20
    Fried Rice 18
Kung Pao Prawns with Cashew Nuts 38
Meat:
    Beef with Broccoli 32
    Pork Chow Mein 24
    Shredded Beef with Vegetables 28
    Spiced Beef 30
    Stir-Fried Calves Liver with Peppers and
        Carrots 26
    Sweet and Sour Pork 22
Noodles:
    Stir-Fry Noodles 20
Pork Chow Mein 24
Poultry:
    Chicken with Walnuts and Celery 34

Prawn Egg Fried Rice 16
Quick Fried Prawns 14
Rice Dishes:
    Fried Rice 18
    Prawn Egg Fried Rice 16
Shredded Beef with Vegetables 28
Singapore Fish 36
Special Mixed Vegetables 40
Spiced Beef 30
Spiced Fried Soup 10
Starters:
    Barbecued Spareribs 12
    Spiced Fried Soup 10
    Wonton Soup 8
Stir-Fried Calves Liver with Peppers and
    Carrots 26
Stir-Fry Noodles 20
Stir-Fry Tofu Salad 42
Sweet and Sour Pork 22
Vegetarian:
    Special Mixed Vegetables 40
    Stir-Fry Tofu Salad 42
Wonton Soup 8

Stir-Fried Calves' Liver with Peppers and Carrots